Classifying Amphibians

KU-417-233

RICHARD AND LOUISE SPILSBURY

Heinemann
LIBRARY

www.heinemann.co.uk/library
Visit our website to find out more information about **Heinemann Library** books.

To order:
☎ Phone 44 (0) 1865 888066
🗎 Send a fax to 44 (0) 1865 314091
💻 Visit the Heinemann Bookshop at www.heinemann.co.uk/library to browse our catalogue and order online.

First published in Great Britain by Heinemann Library, Halley Court, Jordan Hill, Oxford OX2 8EJ, a division of Harcourt Education Ltd. Heinemann is a registered trademark of Harcourt Education Ltd.

Editorial: Jilly Attwood and Jennifer Tubbs
Design: Jo Hinton-Malivoire and AMR
Illustrations: David Woodroofe
Picture Research: Catherine Bevan, Hannah Taylor and Su Alexander
Production: Séverine Ribierre

Originated by Dot Gradations Ltd
Printed in Hong Kong, China by Wing King Tong

ISBN 0 431 16785 0
07 06 05 04 03
10 9 8 7 6 5 4 3 2 1

British Library Cataloguing in Publication Data
Spilsbury, Richard and Louise
Classifying Living Things – Amphibians
597.8'012
A full catalogue record for this book is available from the British Library.

Acknowledgements
For Miles and Harriet, toad enthusiasts.

The publishers would like to thank the following for permission to reproduce photographs: Bruce Coleman: 8 (Jane Burton), 9 (Jane Burton), 11 (Robert Maier), 18 (MPL Fogden); Corbis: 27, 13 (FPLA), 15 (Michael and Patricia Fogden), 17 (Michael and Patricia Fogden), 21 (Kevin Schafer); Digital Stock: 14; Nature Picture Library: 28, 5 (Geoff Dore), 10 (Adrian Davies), 20 (Jim Hallet), 25 (Pete Oxford), 26 (Morley Read); NHPA: 19 (Daniel Heuclin), 23 (T. Kitchin and V. Hurst); Oxford Scientific Films: 7, 22, 4, (Zig Leszczynski), 6 (Mark Hamblin), 12 (M. Wendler/Okapia), 16 (Juan M. Renjifo), 24 (Professor Jack Dermid); RSPCA: 29.

Cover photograph of a society of common frogs in a pond reproduced with permission of the Bruce Coleman Collection (Felix Labhardt).

The publishers would like to thank Catherine Armstrong for her assistance in the preparation of this book.

Every effort has been made to contact copyright holders of any material reproduced in this book. Any omissions will be rectified in subsequent printings if notice is given to the publishers.

Contents

Words in the text in bold, **like this**, are explained in the Glossary.

How classification works

The Earth is populated with an immense variety of living things, from the largest whale to the tiniest insect. Scientists believe that all these **organisms** (living things) are the **descendants** of one group of simple organisms that lived millions of years ago.

Classification can help us to understand how different organisms might be related to each other. It also makes better sense of the great variety of organisms to sort them into groups.

Sorting life

Different living things are grouped according to the characteristics (features) that they have in common. Some are obvious at first glance. For example, any animal you see that has feathers is a bird.

There are many characteristics used to classify organisms that are not so obvious. Fish, mammals, reptiles, birds and amphibians are classified together as they are all **vertebrates** (have an internal backbone). Other less obvious characteristics used to classify organisms include **reproduction** (how they have babies), how they breathe and the type of skin they have.

There are many different ways to classify and scientists often disagree about the best ways. Nevertheless, over time, scientists have come up with a way of sorting all organisms.

The salamander looks a bit like a lizard but it is an amphibian – it has characteristics in common with all other amphibians.

From kingdoms to species

Living things are generally divided into huge groups called kingdoms. Plants, for example, are all grouped in one kingdom, and all animals in another. Each kingdom is divided into smaller groups, each called a **phylum**. A phylum is divided into **classes**, classes into **orders**, orders into **families**, families into **genera** (singular genus) and genera into **species**. A species is a single kind of organism, such as a natterjack toad.

Common and scientific names

Many living things have a common name. Common names are not always exact – for instance, the common toad of Europe is different to a toad that is common in the Sonoran Desert of USA and Mexico.

To sort out such difficulties, scientists give every species a two-part name. The first name is that of the genus the organism belongs to. The second is the name of the species within that genus. Using scientific names, it is easy to tell the two types of toad apart. The common toad has the name *Bufo bufo* and the Sonoran Desert toad is *Bufo alvarius*.

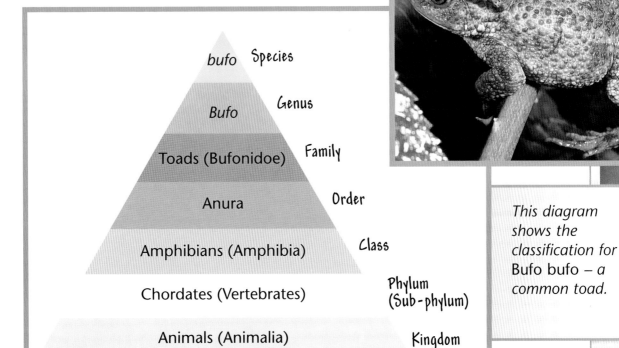

bufo Species

Bufo Genus

Toads (Bufonidoe) Family

Anura Order

Amphibians (Amphibia) Class

Chordates (Vertebrates) Phylum (Sub-phylum)

Animals (Animalia) Kingdom

This diagram shows the classification for Bufo bufo – a common toad.

What is an amphibian?

There are two familiar **orders** in the amphibian **class** – frogs and toads, and newts and salamanders. There is a third, less familiar order called caecilians, which look rather like large worms with teeth. However different these amphibian groups look, they all have several characteristics in common:

- amphibians are **vertebrates** – animals with backbones
- amphibians are cold-blooded, which means their bodies are as warm as their surroundings
- amphibians have naked skin – it has no covering of **scales**, hair or feathers as in other vertebrates
- amphibians **reproduce** using eggs. Young amphibians usually look completely different to adults. They undergo big changes as they develop – this process is called **metamorphosis**.

A final important characteristic is revealed in the name amphibian, which comes from Greek words meaning double life. Amphibians typically spend the early part of their life in water and the later part on land.

The importance of a backbone

A backbone is a tough, flexible rod inside vertebrates. Muscles pull against the backbone to move limbs and other bones. Bones, such as ribs and the skull, connected to the backbone, protect internal organs, like the heart, from damage.

This great crested newt is a member of the Caudata order.

This table shows the orders of amphibians and gives some examples of the main families and species.

Name of order	Families	No. of species	Example
Anura (frogs and toads) Appearance: large head, 4 legs, no tail, longer hind legs	Tailed frogs (Ascaphidae)	2	*Ascaphus truei*
	Toads (Bufonidae)	449	common toad
	Glass frogs (Centrolenidae)	136	emerald glass frog
	Poison-dart frog (Dendrobatidae)	201	strawberry poison-dart
	Treefrogs (Hylidae)	812	White's treefrog
	Southern frogs (Leptodactylidae)	1088	leopard frog
	Mantellas (Mantellidae)	127	golden mantella
	Spadefoot toads (Pelobatidae)	11	plains spadefoot
	Tongueless frogs (Pipidae)	30	*Pipa pipa*
	True frogs (Ranidae)	716	goliath frog
	Mouth-brooding frogs (Rhinodermatidae)	2	*Rhinoderma darwinii*
Caudata (salamanders and newts) Appearance: long body and tail, 4 or 2 equal-sized legs	Mole salamanders (Ambystomatidae)	30	tiger salamander
	Giant salamanders (Cryptobranchidae)	3	hellbender
	Lungless salamanders (Plethodontidae)	352	green salamander
	Mudpuppies and olms (Proteidae)	6	mudpuppy
	Newts and fire salamanders (Salamandridae)	62	great crested newt
	Sirens (Sirenidae)	4	lesser siren
Gymnophiona (Caecilians) Appearance: worm-like body, no legs	Cocle caecilians (Caeciliaidae)	109	rubber eel

The amphibian life cycle

Many different young animals change completely from when they hatch out of the egg to when they become adult. This transformation is called **metamorphosis**. For example, caterpillars are young insects that change into adult butterflies. Amphibians and fish are the only **vertebrates** to change by metamorphosis.

Life in water

Metamorphosis is easiest to see in frogs and toads where the **larvae** (young) – called tadpoles – are a completely different shape to the adults. Adult frogs and toads usually lay their jelly-coated eggs in water or a moist place. When the young tadpoles hatch out of the eggs, they look rather like fish. They have long tails they use for swimming, and **gills** on their sides that allow them to breathe **oxygen** in the water.

Tadpoles change in many ways as they grow up into frogs. Developing legs are an easy change to spot.

*A frog's hind feet have **webbed** toes that it can use for swimming. This tadpole has developed all its legs and is almost ready to leave the water.*

A tadpole's mouth is small, with rows of tiny teeth that it uses to grate bits of water plants to eat. As the tadpole eats more, it grows bigger and starts to change. First it develops hind legs, and then front legs start to appear. Its tail starts to shrink in size and its head, mouth and eyes grow bigger. It begins to look more like an adult toad or frog. It starts to hunt tiny animals in the water to eat and its guts (stomach and intestines) change shape allowing it to digest this new food. The gills transform into **lungs** inside its body.

Life on land

When they eventually crawl out of the water, young frogs and toads are **adapted** in ways that help them in their life on land. Their strong legs allow them to hop and walk around and their tail has mostly disappeared – they do not need it to swim with. They can breathe oxygen in the air using their lungs. Their vision is better in air than in water. This means they can hunt efficiently. Many frogs and toads have a long sticky tongue they can flick out to grab quick-moving food.

Live birth

Metamorphosis also happens in salamanders and caecilians, but it is often less obvious than in frogs. Most caecilians and some salamanders and frogs retain their eggs inside their bodies. The eggs develop safely inside their mothers' bodies. When the larvae emerge from their mothers they are miniature versions of their parents.

Amphibian skin

In wet places, amphibians such as this toad absorb lots of water through their skin. They get rid of some of the excess water by urinating a lot.

Skin without hair, scales or feathers is a characteristic used to help classify animals as amphibians. Thin, bare amphibian skin has both advantages and disadvantages.

Getting enough water

Without the right amount of water, all animals will die. To get the right amount they need to drink, but also control how much water they lose by urination (by weeing) and evaporation from the skin (when water turns from liquid to a gas – a bit like our sweating). For example, reptiles can live in dry places by urinating very little and by having **scales** on their skin, which limits evaporation.

Amphibian skin has no covering to prevent water loss by evaporation. Amphibians hold on to water in their bodies by living in moist places and by producing mucus (slime) from their skin to help keep it moist. Surprisingly, amphibians mostly do not drink. Their thin skin can absorb water very easily from the water, soil or air around them.

Under the skin

Under its outer protective layer, the inner layer of amphibian skin contains nerves, blood vessels (tubes) and **glands**. Glands are places where special fluids are made and released. Some amphibian glands make mucus (slime) but others also make poisons – some lethal, some that just taste bad – to put off **predators**.

Breathing

Amphibians are unusual amongst **vertebrates** as they can use their skin for 'breathing'. **Oxygen** in the air or water around them enters blood vessels beneath the surface of their moist skin. Blood then carries the oxygen to parts of the body that need it. Some salamanders breathe using only their skin, but most amphibians use a combination of skin and either **lungs** or **gills** for breathing, depending on where they live.

Shiny mucus covering the skin of this spotted salamander helps keep the skin moist for breathing through.

Colours

Amphibians are different colours because they have blobs of pigment (special chemicals) in their skin. Colour is vital to many amphibians and other animals for safety. Some are **camouflaged** – predators cannot easily see them because they are a similar colour or pattern to their background. Others are brightly coloured as a warning that they are poisonous – this puts off predators, who know their **prey** will taste bad. Some can even change colour by changing the shape of these pigment blobs. White's treefrogs change colour from green to brown as they move from leaf surfaces to darker backgrounds.

Shedding

After **metamorphosis**, amphibians regularly change their outer skin. This is called shedding. They do this because the skin becomes damaged or too dry. A new layer of skin grows underneath the old one. Toads pull off their old skin like a tight pullover. It does not go to waste – they eat it as a useful food supplement.

Frogs

Frogs are amphibians that do not have tails as adults. They are classified in the same **order** as toads because toads also have no tails as adults. Over 90 per cent of the world's amphibian **species** are frogs and toads. They have so many characteristics in common – such as skeleton shape – that some tailless amphibians are called either toads or frogs.

What is a frog like?

Frogs usually have long, strong hind legs they use for jumping and **webbed** toes that help them swim. Their skin is smooth. They use the bulging, often large eyes on top of their wide heads to see all around. Frogs are the noisiest amphibians. Their sounds are made even louder by areas of skin in their throats, called vocal sacs, that bulge out and act a bit like loudspeakers.

Widespread frogs

Two of the largest **families** of frogs are the true frogs (Ranidae) that contains over 700 species, and the southern frogs (Leptodactylidae) containing over 1000 species. Southern frogs live in Central and South America, the West Indies and southern USA. True frogs live in Africa, the USA, Europe and Asia.

ear

A frog's sensitive ears are hidden under circle-shaped patches of skin, which act like our eardrums.

True frogs

True frogs are called 'true' because they show all the typical frog characteristics – long hind legs, smooth skin and webbed toes. They live in a wide range of **habitats**, from wet to dry and hot to cold. The goliath frog – the biggest frog in the world – lives in West Africa and can measure 30 centimetres long and over 3 kilograms in weight. The bullfrog is an aggressive **predator** that hunts and eats **prey** such as small mammals, fish and ducklings.

The horned frog will eat anything that fits into its enormous mouth. Here it is eating a mouse. Like other frogs and toads it has no teeth to bite or chew, so it can press its eyes down to help swallow large prey.

Southern frogs

Southern frogs also come in lots of different sizes and display typical frog characteristics. The small barking frog gets its name from the call made by males to attract females to **breed**, which sounds rather like a dog barking. Bell's horned frogs are sometimes as big as large dinner plates. They have horn-like knobbles over their skin and striking **camouflage** markings that help them catch their prey.

Frosty frog

Some wood frogs live north of the Arctic circle. They survive freezing winters by hibernating (resting motionless in a special sleep) underground in a burrow. Their bodies do not freeze because the large amount of sugar in their blood acts like antifreeze.

Treefrogs

Several frog **families** spend most of their lives in trees. They are classified as treefrogs because they have special **adaptations** that help them to live among the branches.

Clinging on

Treefrogs (families Hylidae and Hyperoliidae) are mostly less than 10 centimetres long with long, flattened bodies and necks. Treefrogs all have big feet with long toes which help them balance and climb amongst leaves and branches. There is usually a large, flattened disc at the end of each toe. These discs are sticky and help them cling on tightly as they climb. Treefrogs also have cartilage between the last two bones of each toe. This bendy tissue allows the toes to swivel as the frog moves its body, while keeping the toe discs stuck flat against the tree.

The red-eyed treefrog has vertical pupils a bit like a cat's. The pupils open wide at night as it hunts for food such as moths.

Night vision

Many treefrogs are nocturnal – they are active at night and rest during the day. They usually have large eyes that make use of any available light. This allows them to get around, find food and avoid **predators** in trees.

Variety show

Treefrogs live in a variety of places. They mostly live in warm, moist tropical places such as a rainforest, but some live in cooler, drier **habitats** such as Europe. Most treefrogs hunt insects, spiders, centipedes and other small animals to eat, but a few are vegetarian. One Brazilian treefrog eats just fruit!

Many male treefrogs call at night to attract females. Some have common names that describe their call, such as peeper, chorus frog, or bird-voiced frog.

In hiding

Treefrogs are usually the colour of the plants they live amongst. This **camouflages** them so predators cannot spot them. For example, North American treefrogs are bright green because they live amongst bright green plants. They also have patches of yellow on their skin which look like patches of sunlight. This makes them even less visible amongst the leaves.

Odd ones out

Some treefrogs never go near trees but are classified as treefrogs because of certain characteristics such as their skeletons. For example, the water-holding frog that lives in southern Australian deserts spends much of its life hidden underground to avoid the heat. It sheds its protective cocoon (case) of skin when the soil gets wet after rain.

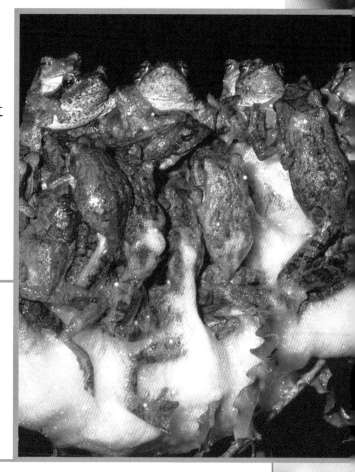

Groups of grey treefrogs lay their eggs in foam nests on branches above streams. The nests, which the frogs make from their own mucus (slime), hide and keep the eggs moist. When the eggs hatch, the larvae drop into the water below.

Other frogs of the forest

The poison in this tiny yellow poison-dart frog is so strong it could kill several humans.

Several other groups of frogs live in or near trees just like treefrogs. They have different ways to help them avoid the attentions of **predators**.

Bright sparks

The poison-dart frogs (**family** Dendrobatidae) of Central and South America and the mantellas (Mantellidae) of Madagascar are very small frogs, less than 5 centimetres long. They live in tropical rainforests. The most striking thing about them is their appearance – some are vivid yellow, others are red with dark stripes, metallic green or even bright blue. Their colours are an **adaptation** – they warn predators that their skin may be poisonous.

Frogs as weapons

Some South American people hunt animals high in trees using blowpipes and darts. They rub the dart tips with poison from a poison-dart frog. When the dart hits an animal, the poison instantly kills it and it drops down to the hunter below.

Poison-dart frogs make poison in special **glands** in their skin. The poison in some frogs is very strong but less so in others. When a predator – such as a bird, snake or spider – starts to eat one, it will at best have a nasty taste in its mouth or at worst be injured by the poison or die. Survivors remember to avoid these colourful frogs in the future.

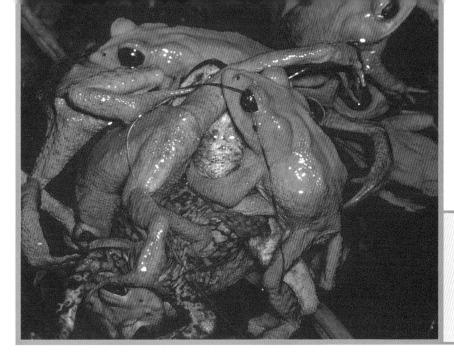

Male mantellas
sometimes wrestle with
each other over control
of places to breed.

Colourful lives

Mantellas and poison-darts also use their colours for other
purposes. In a shady rainforest, a brightly coloured male is
easier for a female to spot. Male mantellas patrol a territory
(their area) that has small pools of water caught inside plants
such as bamboo. After a female is attracted to a colourful male,
she checks out his pools before choosing the right one in
which to lay her eggs.

Females of some poison-dart **species** lay their eggs in nests
made out of leaves on the forest floor. When the eggs hatch,
the females carry their tadpoles to water where they
metamorphose into frogs. Some lay special eggs that have
not been **fertilized** in the water for the tadpoles to feed on.

Flying frogs

Frogs of the family Rhacophoridae also live in trees. Wallace's
flying frog can glide up to 15 metres from one tree to the
next to escape danger. When it jumps, it spreads its large
webbed feet out wide, which stretches the flaps of skin
attached to its sides. The stretched skin forms a sort of
parachute that stops it falling so fast. This means it can get
further away.

Special frog parents

There are four further different groups of frogs that have special ways of caring for their eggs and their young tadpoles.

A tailed frog?

A general characteristic of adult frogs is that they do not have tails, but males of one **family** of frogs do appear to have them! In fact, the 'tail' is a special tube used in **mating**. Tailed frogs (family Ascaphidae) use this unique tube to **fertilize** the female's eggs inside her body. The tube is an **adaptation** to life in rushing streams. In fast-moving water eggs might be washed away before they can be fertilized.

Glass frogs

Glass frogs (family Centrolenidae) get their name because the skin on their bellies is transparent. This is a type of **camouflage** – the colour of the leaves or rocks they rest on shows through their skin, so they cannot easily be seen by **predators**. Some male glass frogs also use this camouflage to hide as they guard their eggs before they hatch. They have spotted skin on their backs so they look a bit like their eggs. If other frogs or small animals approach to eat their eggs they try to chase them off.

You can see the leaf it is resting on through the skin of this glass frog.

Surinam frog
tadpoles hatch out
of protected eggs on
their mother's back.

Throat nursery

Mouth-brooding frogs (family Rhinodermatidae) are a group of small frogs that live in shady forest streams of South America. The female Darwin's frog lays 20 to 30 eggs which the male fertilizes and guards for two weeks. When the eggs are ready to hatch, he appears to eat them! In fact, the tadpoles go into his vocal sacs in his throat rather than his stomach. They remain here, in safe hiding, until they have changed into small frogs. At this point he opens his mouth and they hop away.

Keeping in contact

Tongueless frogs (family Pipidae) are **aquatic** – they always live in water. They suck up food from the muddy riverbeds they live in using their tongueless mouths. The Surinam frog is incredibly flat and looks like a dead leaf. After her sticky eggs are fertilized, the female swims in loops in the water to catch them on her back. Over the next few days, the skin on her back swells around the eggs. This protects them as they develop into tadpoles.

Toads

This natterjack toad is a typical stubby toad shape. Its poison glands are near its eyes.

Toads are classified in the same **order** as frogs. Both have a similar shape with longer hind legs than front legs and no tail, but there are some general differences.

How is a toad different to a frog?

Toads generally have shorter, stubbier bodies than frogs, with thick, dry, warty skin. Behind each eye is a swelling with tiny dimples that contains the toad's poison **glands**. All toads make poison, most of it is not very strong, but only certain frogs do, such as poison-darts. Most toads have fairly drab-coloured skin on their back that **camouflages** them against the ground.

Toad hind legs are usually shorter than those of frogs of similar size and there is little **webbing** between their toes. They crawl slowly and hop whereas frogs swim and leap. Toads generally lay their eggs in sticky strings rather than in clumps like frogs.

True toads

The common European toad is a true toad (family Bufonidae) because it clearly shows toad characteristics. It spends its days resting in shady, sheltered spots. At night it stalks **prey** such as slugs and worms that it catches by flicking out its sticky tongue. If it eats something it does not like the taste of, it can vomit out its stomach and wipe it clean before tucking it back!

Earth movers

Several families of toads have features that help them dig. Spadefoot toads (family Pelobatidae) have tough, spade-shaped feet with hardened pads. They use these to dig backwards into soil, forming burrows. Burrows underground are cool and moist and keep spadefoot toads out of the sight of **predators**.

Narrowmouth toads (family Microhylidae) got their name because their large bellies make their heads look narrow. The Eastern narrowmouth toad of the USA lives in sandy soil that is easy to dig into. It feeds mostly on ants at night, when it is cooler. It can roll forward a fold of skin on its neck to protect its eyes from ant bites and stings.

Advance warning

Many toads put off predators using poison in their skin. Some toads have extra tricks. The fire-bellied toad (family Bombinatoridae) has a green or brown **camouflaged** back but its stomach is bright red or orange. The camouflage hides it from most predators, but if danger gets too close it flashes its tummy. This is a warning to predators to keep away because it is poisonous.

The Mexican burrowing toad (family Rhinophrynidae) blows up like a balloon to look bigger than it really is when alarmed.

spade-shaped back foot

Salamanders

At first sight, most salamanders look like lizards. They have small heads with rows of small teeth, bright skin, long tails and short legs set at right angles to their body. Salamanders, though, are amphibians. Unlike lizards, which are reptiles, they have no scales on their skin, no claws on their toes and they need moist places to **breed** in. Around 500 **species** of salamander have been identified and classified into ten different groups.

The female great crested newt wraps each egg in the leaf of a water plant to hide it until it hatches.

Newts are salamanders

Newts are some of the most familiar salamanders. They are rough-skinned, long-legged members of just one family of salamanders (Salamandridae). Other members of this **family** include the yellow and black fire salamanders.

Male newts put on special displays to attract a female to **breed** with. The male great crested newt, for example, develops a jagged crest along his back, a silver colour on his tail and swims, while waggling his tail in front of the female. This encourages her to lay her eggs, which he then **fertilizes**.

Telling tails

If salamanders are caught by the tail by a **predator**, their tails can drop off so they have a chance to get away. A new tail can grow back. Salamanders can also regrow other damaged or severed parts of their bodies.

Different changes

When fire salamander **larvae** hatch out of their eggs they look similar to their parents. As they grow they do not change much except in size.

Newt larvae look much less like their parents when they hatch. At first they have gills and no legs, rather like tadpoles, but as they grow they change. The front legs then the hind legs soon develop, and the gills transform into **lungs**. After **metamorphosis** the young newt leaves the water to live on land until it is old enough to **reproduce**.

Heavy build

Mole salamanders (family Ambystomatidae) are from North America. They all have robust bodies, blunt heads, small eyes and flattened tails. They get their name from their good digging abilities. At up to 40 centimetres long the tiger salamander is the largest salamander that lives on land. It comes out at night and uses its good sense of smell to hunt worms, mice, insects and other amphibians.

Tiger salamander larvae are just over 1 centimetre long when they hatch. They eat so much that they get ten times bigger over the next twelve weeks.

Second change

Just after metamorphosis, Eastern newts are called efts. An eft has bright red skin as a warning to **predators** about the poison it contains. After several years growing up on land, the eft changes colour to brown and develops a flattened tail that it uses for swimming. Although still poisonous, it is then an adult ready to return to the water to breed.

Aquatic and lungless salamanders

Other salamanders can be divided into two main sorts – **aquatic** and lungless. Aquatic salamanders always live in or next to water, but lungless salamanders live in a variety of damp **habitats**.

Eternal youth

Adults of many of the aquatic salamander **families** look the same as their **larvae**. Grown-up mudpuppies and olms (family Proteidae) have feathery **gills** on their sides and **fins** at the top and bottom of their tail. They have the same features that help them to breathe and swim as their larvae because they also live in water. The olm lives in pools in dark caves. It is blind, has pinkish-white skin and a long snout that it uses to smell **prey** such as worms.

Adult hellbenders and giant salamanders (family Cryptobranchidae) have gills inside their bodies, hidden behind slits. These amphibians have wide heads and wrinkled fleshy skin. They live in fast-flowing, rocky rivers and shelter in long burrows under river banks.

Sirens (family Sirenidae) have long eel-like bodies and just two (front) legs. Unlike other aquatic salamanders, they have both gills and **lungs** after **metamorphosis**.

Mudpuppies never transform entirely. They reach 20 to 45 centimetres long, but do not lose their red gills during their lives.

Without lungs

There are around 350 species of lungless salamander (family Plethodontidae). Most live in North and Central America. They do not have lungs or gills. Instead, they breathe through their skin and the lining of their mouth. Most lungless salamanders are quite small – less than 15 centimetres long. A few **species** live permanently in water, but most live in damp places on land, near streams, among moss or under stones.

Lungless salamanders eat small prey such as insects, slugs and woodlice. Adults usually feed at night and spend the daytime hiding. Most lungless salamanders can see quite well but they usually find their prey by sensing vibrations from the ground. They also use their keen senses of smell and taste, which they feel through their sensitive tongue. The shasta salamander can shoot out its long sticky tongue almost the full length of its body to catch prey such as flies.

High and low

Lungless salamanders can live in very different places. Some live in caves or wells, 60 metres underground. Others live in trees, as high as 15 metres above the ground.

The arboreal salamander (a lungless salamander) climbs trees using broad, flat, **webbed** feet and a prehensile (gripping) tail. It makes its home in old birds' nests.

Caecilians

Caecilians (pronounced 'kye-killi-uns') are amphibians that never have legs. They look a bit like worms or snakes but are classified as amphibians because of characteristics such as smooth, slimy skin with no scales. Caecilian skin forms tough raised rings along their long, thin bodies.

There are over 150 **species** of caecilians in five groups. Most are black or pale, although some are brightly coloured. Caecilians range in size from just a few centimetres to over a metre long and they live in warm places, such as Mexico, South-east Asia and parts of Africa.

Going underground

Most types of caecilian live in burrows underground. They usually burrow headfirst into soft earth, forcing a path with their hard skull. The rings on their body, like those on an earthworm, help them get a grip as they move through the soil.

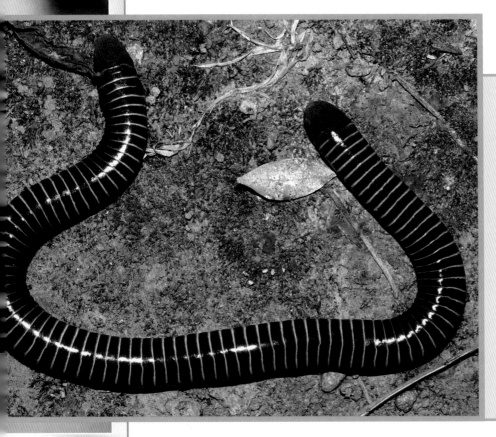

This blue caecilian looks a bit like a large earthworm. Unlike worms, caecilians have a skeleton inside their body and teeth inside their jaws. They also have a tentacle beneath the eyes – a sense organ that helps them detect prey in their dark burrows.

Caecilians' small eyes are usually covered with skin, and often by bone, too, so they are nearly blind.

The lives of caecilians

Because caecilians live most of their lives underground, it is hard for scientists to study them in detail. Caecilians only come to the surface when they have to, to escape drowning if rain floods their burrow for example.

Caecilians are carnivores (meat-eaters), eating small underground **prey** such as earthworms and termites. Their main **predators** are large, burrowing snakes. Caecilians are thought to live alone most of the time, coming together only to **mate**.

Male caecilians, unlike other male amphibians, **fertilize** the female's eggs inside her body. **Larvae** of many species hatch from the eggs inside their mother and are then born live. Other caecilians lay eggs in nests and guard their eggs and young carefully.

Caecilian divers

Fishermen in the muddy waters of South American rivers often catch the **aquatic** caecilians, commonly called 'rubber eels'. They have flat bodies and a small tail **fin**, so they are often mistaken for fish called eels. Their skin is wrinkly and provides a large enough surface for skin-breathing in the muddy water.

Pioneers of water and land

The first **vertebrates** to live on land were amphibians. Scientists believe that over 350 million years ago – well before dinosaurs walked the earth – a few fish started to crawl out of the sea using their **fins**. On the wet mud they could catch lots of insects to eat and then go back into the water. Over time their **descendants adapted** in ways that allowed them to live on land. Eventually they became so different to fish that we consider them to be a different type of animal – amphibians. These amphibians, like those of today, returned to the water when it was time to breed. Their eggs and **larvae**, like those of fish, could only develop properly if moist.

One of a kind

Amphibians are a unique class of vertebrates. Although the class contains a wide range of different shapes and sizes, they all have a distinct combination of the characteristics that make them amphibians.
Other groups of animals may have one of these characteristics, but no other group has all of them together.

Eels are very similar in shape to caecilians. However, unlike amphibians, eels have scales on their skin, gills and many other fish characteristics.

Tricky classification

Classifying amphibians is not always straightforward. For example, mole salamanders look like lizards called skinks. But, on closer inspection, skinks unlike salamanders have dry, **scale**-covered skin. But classifying animals based just on one characteristic – skin – can be difficult. For example, some lizard **species** have very smooth skin with scales so tiny they are difficult to see and so they could be mistaken for amphibians. Individual animals also vary, just like humans. Some amphibians are differently sized, differently coloured or differently shaped from others in the same species.

Examining a range of characteristics is necessary for classification because some amphibians do things differently. As we have seen through this book, some frogs lay their eggs on land, not in water, and some salamanders never **metamorphose**. But all amphibians have more characteristics in common with each other than with any other type of animal.

Same solution

Different types of animals often look the same because they have the same features that help them to live in the same **habitat**. For example, caecilians look a bit like big worms. Both animals have smooth, slippery skin, segment rings and are blind because they both spend their lives burrowing through the soil.

Glossary

adaptation special feature that helps an organism to survive in its particular habitat

aquatic living in water

breed produce young

camouflage colour, shape or pattern that disguises an animal against its background

class classification grouping. The amphibian class contains three orders.

descendant later generation of organism

family classification grouping. Each order is made up of many families.

fertilize when male sex cells join with female sex cells (eggs) so they can develop into larvae

fin flap of skin with or without bones in it that helps an animal swim

genus (plural **genera**) classification grouping. Each family is made up of many genera.

gill structure used for breathing underwater

gland part of an animal's body that produces and releases particular fluids

habitat type of place where an organism lives

larva (plural **larvae**) amphibian young

lung body structure found in most vertebrates, used for breathing in air

mate produce young

metamorphosis process of change from larva shape to adult shape

order classification grouping. There are three orders of amphibians.

organism living thing

oxygen gas used by most organisms to breathe

phylum classification grouping. Each phylum is divided into different classes.

predator animal that hunts and eats other animals

prey animal that is hunted and eaten by another animal

reproduce have babies

scales overlapping or interlocking pieces that form a protective layer over reptile and fish skin

species classification grouping. There are often several species within each genus.

vertebrate animal with an internal backbone

webbed when an animal has skin stretched between its toes so its feet can be used like paddles

Further resources

Books

DK Handbook: Reptiles and Amphibians, Mark O'Shea and Tim Halliday (Dorling Kindersley, 2001)

Eyewitness Guides: Amphibian, Barry Clarke (Dorling Kindersley, 1993)

Life Processes: Classification, Holly Wallace (Heinemann Library, 2000)

What's the difference?: Amphibians, Stephen Savage (Hodder Wayland, 2002)

Websites

http://allaboutfrogs.org/weird/weird.html
Weird frog facts.

http://cgee.hamline.edu/frogs/science/faq2.html#unusua
Frequently and infrequently asked questions about frogs.

http://elib.cs.berkeley.edu/aw/lists/index.shtml
Amphibiaweb: detailed information about all the amphibian families.

www.reptilepark.com.au/animals/amphibians/index/html
Find out about Australian amphibians, where they like to live, what they eat and how they behave.

Index